COSTLY MISTAKES IN CHRISTIAN COURTSHIP

KANYINSOLA HELEN COLE
OLORI, ADERONKE OYENIYI, PhD

Published in Nigeria by
RIGHTWAY PUBLISHERS
1, Dada Estate Road, Osogbo,
Osun State, Nigeria.

ISBN Ebook: 978-978-982-179-2

Osun State, Nigeria.

ISBN PAPERBACK: 978-978-982-178-5

All the scripture quotations, unless otherwise indicated are taken from the **Holy Bible,** *King James Version, and New Living Translation*

COSTLY MISTAKES IN CHRISTIAN COURTSHIP

oyin.helencole@gmail.com & oyeniyironke@gmail.com
Blog Address: Nikkyella.com
Edited by Adedolapo Ayobami

CONTENTS

Foreword

It is a great honour to write a foreword to this piece of work.

You don't need to be told that this book is a masterpiece when you cross-check the biographies of the authors. The duo is academia and a combination of the experience of people who have seen it all –the elderly and successfully married woman spanning beyond four decades and a young lady whom I can easily call the new school. The combinations of the old school and the new school would definitely produce the future school. Marriage is the 'Future school' the world is waiting for (heaven on earth experience). Not only that, I made bold to say that Mama Olori and her daughter-partner Kanyinsola in this great work, are not babes in Christendom. Their long-term relationship with God and understanding of the scriptures form a strong pillar that sustains the richness of this great book.

How I wished a book of this importance were written some couple of years back, immediately the western culture and civilisation crept into our well-laid down traditional ways of marriage and infiltrated our ways of doing things negatively. All intended partners got a copy before the wedding. I said this because most probably, many unfulfilled couples we see today with the untold crises would have long been separated and parted ways and not get married to the individual. Remember this saying, "broken courtship is better than broken homes." And here we are today with a high rate of broken marriages, sad and unhappy couples with faces of partners showing regrets. I equally believe that the rate of domestic violence would have reduced drastically if at all, we have any.

Many marriages started with "I am pregnant." In contrast, others began with "yes I do" Only a few understand the significance of courtship in the marriage process. To some, it is a time of fun, going to parties, visiting, adventure, and the making of love. No, I am not saying it is a time of dull moments, but it goes beyond all that.

This masterpiece in your hand intends to take you to a voyage of discovery.

If the concept of courtship is not necessary for marriage, couples would have been joined together the same day, an agreement is made to become husbands and wives. It is a time of stock-taking. A period when you have the opportunity to cross-examine your decision and get convinced that the two of you are meant for each other, compatible, and fit to form a great future together. Luke 14: 28-32;

"For which of you intending to build a tower, does not sit down first and count the cost, whether he has enough to finish it Lest after he

has laid the foundation, and is not able to finish, all who see it begin to mock him, Saying, 'this man began to build and was not able to finish'? Or what king, going to make war against another king, does not sit down first and consider whether he is able with ten thousand to meet him who comes against him with twenty thousand? Or else, while the other is still a great way off, he sends a delegation and asks conditions of peace."

Therefore, I call courtship a lens. It is a lens through which you clearly see the future, giving you foresight and insight into what you will see in your partners and what the future holds for you both in your intending home.

My long experience as a pastor and a marriage counsellor has shown vividly that many homes are formed on the surface without digging deep; resulting in statements like "had I known, I would not have married somebody like you!" "how did I get involved in a relationship with an unfortunate person like you?" "I know I am smart," definitely you used diabolic power (super force) on me" "how I wished I considered it very well before I went into it" "Pastor, I made a mistake!"

For you not to make mistakes, this comprehensive and detailed book is taking you through the real meaning of courtship, all that it entails for every young man and woman to "shine their eyes" before saying "I do."

I, therefore, congratulate Mama Olori, Olufi of Gbonganland, and her Daughter, Sister Kanyinsola Helen Cole, on this successful publication. Well-done!

PASTOR KAYODE HEPHZIBAH OYEJOBI,

PRESIDENT,

THE RIGHTEOUS PATH MINISTRIES, SOUGHT OUT ASSEMBLY

GBONGAN, OSUN STATE, NIGERIA.

ACKNOWLEDGEMENTS

We appreciate God, the author, and finisher of our faith, who made it possible for us to write this book. We acknowledge Him for inspiration and revelation. The scripture says with men, this is impossible, but with God, all things are possible.

We appreciate Pastor Oyejobi Kayode for his immeasurable support in ensuring the success of this book, without which we would still be scribbling on a rough draft. He has been incredible. We also wish to thank Pastor Greater Oyejobi for proofreading this piece of work and for your counsel, thank him his constant encouragement. We thank Mr Adedolapo Ayobami for editing this piece. He is our major editor. We also thank him for his professional advise.

We appreciate His Royal Majesty Oba, Dr Adetoyese Oyeniyi, Odugbemi I for proofreading and editing this piece. We acknowledged Couples who took time to respond to our questionnaires and those who granted us access to interview and probe into the deep part of their marital life, an act only a few could do.

We appreciate Our father-in-the-Lord, Dr Daniel Kolawole Olukoya, and our mentors: Pastor Wale Peter Osho, Pastor Oyejobi Kayode, Pastor Sebastian, Pastor Adebayo Durojaiye, Pastor Oyejobi Greater, Pastor Daniel Subuloye, Pastor Niyi Alaka, Pastor Opeyemi Omoniyi, Pastor Babatunde.

We would love to appreciate ourselves, I (Dr Oyeniyi), for always proofreading and pointing out errors Kanyinsola did not see. I thank Kanyinsola for typing this and always editing this piece. It's an excellent work.

We also acknowledge everyone who took part in ensuring the book comes out well.

DEDICATION

We dedicate this book to all youths.

We hope it helps you find God's will and mandate in your Courtship, which is a preparatory stage for a godly marriage.

AUTHORS' INSIGHT

The Bible in Proverbs 4:5 says: *"get wisdom and get understanding."* Proverbs 1:7: *"says the fear of the LORD is the beginning of knowledge, but fools despise wisdom and instruction."*

The above portions of the scriptures quickly suggest that any wisdom and understanding outside God is foolishness. It is, therefore, of a necessity for a youth hoping to live in the fullness of God's purpose in life to get the right knowledge that comes only from God.

It is on this note that I, (Dr Aderonke) wish to let you know that one of God's ways in establishing His purpose for your life is marriage, I can authoritatively affirm this because I've been married for over Four Decades. However, the "means" to this "end" (Marriage) is as crucial and essential as marriage itself. It may not be an error to say that once the "means" is right, we are almost sure of the correctness of the "end." The "means" entails several items, including finding the right partner and living wisely from the time of seeing to the time of solemnisation. The later, commonly known as Courtship, requires the proper wisdom and understanding. It is wisdom to take one's time to learn about what you are getting yourself into correctly, or if you are already in it, it is wise to understand God's expectation over your Courtship.

Some false doctrines and teachings are capable of misleading one. If you are not careful enough to know the mind of God in Courtship, you might end up in a mess. Like Moses cried out to God in Exodus 33:13: "*Now, therefore, I pray thee, if I have found grace in thy sight, shew me now thy way, that I may know thee, that I may find grace in thy sight: and consider that this nation is thy people.*" God answered him in verse 14: "*and he said, My presence shall go with thee, and I will give thee rest.*" If the presence of God is not in your Courtship, you can rest assured are heading for destruction.

Proverb 1:5 says, "*a wise man will hear and will increase learning, and a man of understanding shall attain unto wise counsel.*" This book, therefore, seeks to provide you with the right counsel you need for your Courtship to be in-line with the will of God. It is a book on how to have the ideal God-designed and heaven-bound Courtship, which is a good foundation for a Christian home.

INTRODUCTION

Before we wrote this manuscript, I (Dr Aderonke) have had several sessions with intending and married couples, sharing Insights and giving godly counsel and motherly advice. I've had to intervene in disputes settling among both locals and well-educated minds. All this I do regularly as a marriage counsellor, Lecturer, Trainer, and as a Queen. Some of the insights are included in the chapters which you will discover as you read through.

The thought to do this didn't occur to me (Dr Aderonke) until my daughter (Kanyinsola), after she ended what I call a "toxic relationship," walked into my room, sat next to me, and proposed this piece you're reading. I didn't pay much attention to her (Kanyinsola) until She started the manuscript, which I joined in the same year 2018. At first, she (Dr Aderonke) laughed hysterically, somehow, I (Kanyinsola) managed to win Dr Aderonke over after several sessions of convincing words and sharing Case – studies which are the reality of our time and society. Of a truth, it is a subject matter to take a pause long enough to shine the spotlight on, I (Dr Aderonke) remember some cases I've had to intervene ranging from parental influence, betrayal of trust, Educational background, among others.

As we commenced writing, she (Kanyinsola) was elated, and I (Dr Aderonke) was delighted because I know her ideas had the potential for helping those who are in a relationship and those who are about going into it find direction and guidance. We hope you will hear our voices harmonising as one and our hearts beating as one to communicate a message, we believe will impact you significantly.

Two years later, after articulating our knowledge and research, we have now written this book, "Costly mistakes in Christian Courtship." We believe this book will give you some insights, if not all, as we deliberately present our ideas in a way, we think you would find it easy to relate with. In the first and half of this book, we seek to explain the need for courtship. In the second half of the book will help you know what to steer clear of and guidelines to make your courtship smart darts that strike at places that matter. The concluding part will help you understand ingredients you mustn't miss out in making your courtship worthwhile.

The book is enriched by our wide terrain of experience and perspectives.

CHAPTER ONE

WHY YOU SHOULD READ THROUGH

When I (Kanyinsola) was in secondary school, Mathematics was not one of the subjects I liked. Once the teacher comes into the class, I would immediately begin to sleep. I had a phobia for figure Up till my undergraduate days. I had a breakthrough the moment I spoke with the lecturer, teaching me "Risk management." I remember her words, she said: "calculation is actually the easiest course to study provided you follow the principle." She gave me the principle to solve Return on investment (ROI). So I picked up my pen and began to solve it, I began to follow the principle, at first, I didn't arrive at the right answer, so I looked through the principle again to see where I got it wrong. I figured the step I missed, and I started to solve the problem still. This time, I did it more patiently. As I unravelled the equation, I arrived at the right answer. Courtship can be compared to my analogy and the guiding principles. I'm sure you are aware that each topic in calculation has principles guiding it. Imagine if I had applied the wrong principle to solve the problem I stated above. I will never arrive at the right answer.

There are principles guiding life, i.e., ranging from walking with God, passing an examination, having a financial breakthrough. In walking with God, we must be holy (*Follow peace with all men, and holiness, without which no man shall see the Lord*, Hebrews 12:14) righteousness and purity of heart are cogent with walking with God. As a student, to excel, you must labour in studying (*Study to shew thyself approved unto God, a workman that needeth not to be ashamed, rightly dividing the Word of truth. But shun profane and vain babblings: for they will increase unto more ungodliness*, II Timothy 2:15). I believe this principle has not changed. Although I observed that some people try to replace this principle for praying. Also, in the case of knowing the will of God and having a courtship that will lead to marriage, principles are guiding it. If you observe that your Courtship is not working, check the level of your obedience toward the laid down principles of Courtship in the Word of God.

Although it took a while before I realised all these principles. I had made mistakes in Courtship; it was only by the grace of God; I didn't miss it maritally. As you read through this book, you will discover the principles. Why should you care to read through and apply the principles? Several years ago, my mother told me that the moment I (Kanyinsola) set out to go to a particular place or do a specific thing, I should ask those that have gone through it successfully. As I advanced in age, the reality of her words began to dawn on me, I'm sure that the significant reader of this book is about to be in courtship or those already in it. By default, the vast majority of your future in courtship is my past because I (Dr Oyeniyi) am married. If I have gone through it, it means I have experience, knowledge, and revelation of it. No experience should be slightly considered. It is said that history often repeats itself, why?

Because no one cares to listen, to avoid making the same mistakes I made in the past, it will be to your best interest to learn from me. Another question you should ask is, can a blind lead a blind? *(And he spoke a parable unto them, Can the blind lead the blind? Shall they not both fall into the ditch?* Luke 6: 39) how do you know that someone is blind in a particular area? When His or Her life is not showing the result of what they say. I have seen some people who talk about courtship but are not an exemplary display of what they say.

Of a truth, there are no authorities in the subject matter of Courtship, there are experts in it that have what it takes to lead you to succeed in it. But success will only happen when you obey the principles in-line with the word of God to the letter. In the next chapters, the light will be shed on the need for Courtship, Major things that must be done in Courtship, Mistakes Singles make in Courtship.

CHAPTER TWO

THE NEED FOR MARRIAGE

As you advance in age, education, career, life calling, and other pursuits of life, as an unmarried youth, nature, and circumstances around you necessitate you to look out for someone you would want to share and spend the rest of your life with. It is God's design for humanity, and it is not out of scope, provided you have not been called into Celibacy (Matthew 19:12). God said in Genesis "it is not suitable for the man to be alone, and I will make a help meet for him." It gives a reason for marriage. As marriage is for companionship, something unexplainable in man cries out for companionship and the need for a partner. Marriage is also for procreation as it is the only supported atmosphere for Children of God for having sexual intercourse and raising godly children. Marriage is God's institution, and He desires that a man be not alone.

Marriage is more than a relationship because it is encompassing all aspects of life. Although there are critical areas of life in which we must not fail; our fellowship with God (prayers, fasting, Bible study and other necessary ingredients required for spiritual growth), career, service to humanity, social services, ministry, among many others, marriage is ranked first on this list. About (70%) of the success of a man or woman largely depends on who they marry. Marriage is the foundation on which our intellectual, emotional, social, spiritual, and physical aspects of life are built on.

Marriage is therefore, the coming together of a man and a woman to build a home. Marriage is the institution God himself established. Marriage is meant for mature men that is spirit-filled, God-fearing, who understands the need for a wife and has realised God's purpose for their lives. It is also not meant for a girl that believes in living her life the way she wants but for a woman. It is so because marriage comes with several responsibilities and challenges that can only be handled by mature minds.

Gary Chapman, in his book on five love languages, opined that the social institution of marriage is first and foremost a covenant relationship in which a man and a woman pledge themselves to each other for a lifetime partnership. He further explained that at the heart of marriage, therefore, is the idea of unity. It is the opposite of aloneness.

For this reason, the man that God has given the grace to marry is a person that is matured enough to know that he is ripe to take care of another person and see the person as part of himself. When such a man discovers that and his mind is ready to follow God's instruction and direction, he is then prepared to go into a relationship as directed by God.

As he takes the step of faith, God arranges the bone of his bone that will be interested and be ready to go into the same relationship (courtship). Courtships divinely orchestrated and directed by God ensures that the coming of a man and a woman together is without doubts and struggles.

Marriage can be explained as and compared to an earthly building; if a building is to remain firm and withstand turbulent winds, the foundation has to be very strong. Such is the case of Marriage; the foundation must be substantial (consider Luke 14:34).

Courtship before Marriage is a process that requires not missing any of the steps before marriage comes in, which are the proposal, acceptance, and the beginning of the courtship. This should not be done on behalf of any of the parties as it is traditionally believed. Anyone who misses any of the processes is bound to stumble and regret that singular act.

Courtship is not blind to individual interest; this is to say a proposal made on behalf of someone without the person involved may end up in regret. It is because individual differences cannot be eliminated in courtship (even in Christendom, matchmaking is common). We don't have to be sentimental about it because it's a lifelong matter, and each individual has his or her own taste.

Marriage is, therefore, a purposeful, intimate, complementary, committed, and united relationship between a man and a woman, with God as the common ground.

Kindly follow through as we carefully look into what Courtship actually entails in the light of the scriptures.

CHAPTER THREE

WHAT IS COURTSHIP?

Upon the proposal of marriage by a man and subsequent acceptance by the woman, courtship begins. Courtship is the final stage of Marriage. It is the gap between the time you say "yes, I will do," and when you finally say "yes, I do," before God and other witnesses. It is the period in which the two partners involved come together and agree to do away with bad habits they have accumulated over the years and also share good virtues together. Courtship is basically a time for agreement and for reaching consensus on various matters.

Courtship is the vehicle that should transport the parties involved to the real thing called **marriage**. It is a period for you to weigh and check if you would still love to continue the relationship before tying the nut. It is time you can always exit the relationship before you get into the marriage. Once you are married, you mustn't even think about divorce, as God hates it. A broken courtship is better than a broken marriage. A broken marriage will leave a permanent scar on you; it will also leave you in shambles except Jesus picks up the pieces of your life and redesign it. A broken marriage is terribly unfortunate, and it's uncalled for in Christendom.

Courtship is a time to learn about your individual differences, a time to accommodate your partner; it's basically a time to learn about each other. **Amos 3:3** says, *"can two people walk together except they agree?"* Courtship is, therefore, the weaving period of a cord that will bind two people together. Hence, it has to be strong enough to take them far into marriage and after that.

Before you consider going into marriage, there is a need for spiritual, mental, physical, financial maturity, and emotional stability. It is a foolish thing to get into a marriage without all of these. You can build these during courtship.

CHAPTER FOUR

WHY COURTSHIP IS ESSENTIAL

It was in the garden of Eden that God created Eve for Adam with good intention that what God has created was just perfect for Adam and for being the first family on earth. When the problem ensued, Genesis 3:12, Adam said: "*The woman whom thou gavest to be with me, she gave me of the tree, and I did eat.*" This means if Adam had gone through courtship, he could have understood the nature of Eve and how to nurture her according to God's commandment.

- For a deeper understanding of who your partner is
- For a close observation
- To know the principles and norms influencing your partner
- To tell your partner's things you don't want from him/her

- To become close friends
- To learn to walk together and react together, to ensure a link of the chain that is stronger than iron
- To spend quality time together
- To pray together
- To set robust spiritual, financial, and material strategies
- To know some foundational truth about your partner
- To know your partner past, present and plan a future together
- To discover the uniqueness and potential of your partner
- To spend time studying the Word of God together
- To discover things that interest your partner
- To come to a leverage
- To discover and understand your individual differences
- To know areas to pray about
- To seek clarification of some things you don't understand about your partner
- To ask intelligent questions and also, to watch and pray.

1.   For a deeper understanding of who your partner is:

You must not assume that because you met the brother or sister in the church, then you don't need to court because you think they are reasonable, matured, heaven-bound, God-fearing, intelligent, smart, wise, etc., you must assume nothing. Assumption is a costly mistake that can make you utter statements like "had I known" when you finally get married. Some brothers and sisters are good pretenders, they can feign their behaviour and you may end up going with a counterfeit belief of their reality. It takes a close watch and observation to understand who your partner really is. In case you don't know, there are wolves in the house of God! Even Jesus had to chase away those buying and selling in the church of God. The mistakes many people make is this after they must have discovered a terrible thing about their partner, instead of discontinuing the relationship, they continue with the excuse of "I love him/her deeply" or "he/she loves me deeply." Listen, if you stay on this basis, you are heading for regrets.

2.	For close observation:

Courtship is for close observation of how your intending spouse reacts when angry, including words he/she utters and other things. Observe whether he/she is the exact type, whether he/she is organised, whether he/she takes God seriously, whether he/she is God-fearing. Remember, you cannot observe someone you aren't close to.

3.	To know the principles and norms influencing your partner:

We all have different family backgrounds. Therefore, we have some esteemed principles, norms, values, and other themes that guide and influence our decision making. You must understand this very well. The fact that your partner is from the same language speaking culture doesn't necessarily mean there are no distinguishing factors. You must know who influences your intending spouse. By this, I mean who your intending spouse relates with. You must know his role model. If his role model has four wives, there are all possibilities he will become like his role model. Who is her role model? If her role model is a divorcee or one who does not believe in marriage and submission to her husband, she might likely be like her role model. Who is his mentor? If his mentors have divorced about six times, he might become like that. Who are the people she listens to? the truth is people do not always outgrow the circle of friends they walk with. The truth is there are some people that, if you listen to them, your life might be in everlasting confusion. If you listen to the wrong person, you will act wrongly.

4.   To spend quality time together:

This is one reason why people get married for companionship. You need to spend quality time together to get along. Time to share your experiences together, time to know the man/woman you are about to get married to. By spending quality time together, you will be able to tell if he has a mind of his own, whether he can preside over issues, and know if he can protect you.

5.   To pray together:

You need to pray along with your partner. No matter how tight your schedule may be. This is really important. Prayer is how we communicate with God, and he communicates with us too. Praying together creates an atmosphere where the Holy Spirit thrives better. Praying partners lose anger, ego, greed, depression, insecurity, and fear of death in prayer. Prayer sometimes is not about gaining but losing. Losing our Adamic nature, when you continually engage the spirit, certain things will leave your spirit-man Prayer is a two-way thing. We lose selfishness, and we get things from God. The devil always fights against any union that will depopulate his kingdom. The only way to resist him is through prayer. James 4:7

6.   To set robust spiritual, financial, and material strategies:

Jesus said, no man will want to build a house and will not first sit down and count the cost; this implies strategies. A strategy is a plan of action intended to accomplish a specific goal. You must learn to stay ahead of situations; the only way is to set a realisable strategy that will help you. We must not be foolish in courtship. Don't involve yourself in anything without having plans. For you to be successful in life, you need to develop strategies that would help you achieve those desired goals.

7.   To know some foundational truth about your partner:

There are some family trends, patterns, and the likes that you must know about your partner. These foundational truths must not be hidden so you can know areas to which you direct your prayers., so you won't be a bat Christian who can't see.

8.   **To know about your partner's past present, and then plan a future together:**

Our lives are a part of our voyage that started long ago. Every saint has a past, and every sinner has a future. No matter how holy you might appear to be, you still would have a history. Courtship is the right time to reveal your past. Talk about your past, but make sure you are not even living in the past. *I (Kanyinsola) learn of a brother who was in a relationship with a sister, he told the sister of his horrible past (fornication) with past girlfriends. While they were still courting, he was found fornicating with one of his EX-girlfriends. His Fiancé discontinued under the resolve that the brother has a sexual problem that even Marriage cannot solve.* Premarital Sex obstructs God's plan for one's life. Living in fornication is not the right way you are not married. Courtship is the period to tell your partner of things you regret to have done in the past. The Bible says, *"Therefore, if any man is in Christ, he is a new creature; old things are passed away; behold, all things have become new"* (I Cor 5:17). Your past should be a past indeed.

9.   **To spend time studying the word of God together:**

"In the beginning was the Word, and the Word was with God, and the Word was God. The same was in the beginning with God" (John 1:1-2). By studying the Word of God together, it means you are learning about God and his ways. You need to learn about Him properly. John 10:4 says, *"And when he putteth forth his own*

sheep, he goeth before them, and the sheep follow him: for they know his voice."

Verse 5 continued to say: "And a stranger will they not follow but will flee from him: for they know not the voice of strangers." By studying Him, you are learning to recognise his voice, and any voice that's different from His you will detect.

"And they overcame him by the blood of the lamb and by the word of their testimony, and they loved not their lives unto the death." (Revelation 12:11); the Word of God earns us victory and testimonies. This is the power and efficacy of His Word.

"For the word of God is quick, and powerful, and sharper than any two-edged sword, piercing even to the dividing asunder of soul and spirit, and of the joints and marrow, and is a discerner of the thoughts and intents of the heart." (Hebrew 4:12). The Word of God pierces through the soul and spirit; it reveals deep things about your partner.

10.   To discover things that interest your partner:

Different things interest different people. Some love music, others don't. Some are extroverts, while others are introverts. Some love reading, others don't. Don't be tempted to think that it doesn't matter. It does matter. If you neglect this aspect, it might be a problem in the future. After you must have discovered this, it is therefore essential that both of you come to leverage, reach a consensus such that one partner's interests do not affect the other, that individuality be encouraged.

11. To discover and understand your individual differences:

It is imperative to understand your differences, understand what differentiates you from your partner, and accept the differences. Do not have low self-esteem. Individual differences are not to make one party less of a person but to allow you to discover your uniqueness and your area of strengths and weaknesses.

12. To seek clarification of some things you don't understand about your partner: After Jesus spoke to the multitude in parables, his disciples privately met him for clarification. There are some things that you might not understand on the surface level, it is, therefore, essential to clarify.

13. To ask questions and also, to watch and pray:

It is essential to ask questions about your partner's health, family traits, educational background, the type of job your partner does, his/her dream life, and some other intelligent questions. The saying "Like mother, like daughter, like father, like son" is not a myth. You must have a clear understanding of each other's parental model. One of the things that should be done during courtship is making a list of the stuff of lousy habits/traits in your mother or father that you do not like and begin to pray and work against them. Failure to do this might bring a repeated negative partner in your proposed home.

CHAPTER FIVE

TYPE OF PARTNERS

While courting, there are things to note; you must know the kind of person you are courting. You must take note of things that are happening to you positively or negatively during the courtship. You must begin to take note of everything. Take note if your spiritual life is dying gradually during the cause of the courtship if you are always falling sick, take note of everything.

Note: *If all that has been happening to you since you started the courtship is mostly negative, and there is little or no progress in your life, then you need to put the relationship on hold, pray well and seek godly counsel, for this may be an indication that you are courting the wrong person.*

There is a story of a sister that got to me; the sister always had a sleepless night, fatigue, headache, loss of appetite, heart pain, and she is internally troubled. Each time she remembers she is in a relationship, fear grips her heart, and she is not always happy. Then, she told a counsellor, and she was advised not to pick the brother's call for three days. She obliged, and she had peace of mind, no heartache, no fear, and other abnormal things that usually happen to her. Then, she realised that the reason she had sleepless nights was because of the wrong relationship she was in. Thank God she eventually broke the connection.

I like you to carefully consider the following on different types of partners

1.   Caterpillar Partner

If you want a clear picture of what/how your marriage will look like, observe your courtship. If, during your courtship, you notice that all the ethical, moral conducts, the godly ethics, and values you have declined. Your prayer life, Bible study life, your life goals, potentials, and others are no more, my advice is for you to FLEE! This is simply a danger signal that you are courting a caterpillar partner.

2.   Parasite Partner

Parasite, as defined by the dictionary, is an organism that lives on or in another organism, deriving benefit from living on or in that other organism, while not contributing towards its host sufficiently to cover the cost One party is giving while the other party is not committing a quota/ adding value to the life of the other party - that is not reciprocal.

Parasite partner is a partner who lives on other people's efforts or expenses and gives little or nothing back. A lot of marriages would not have taken place, they would have saved themselves of the marital distress they are going through, if only they had been careful to take note of all of these. Life is a balance between holding and letting go. Do not continue to hold on to that relationship if your spirit is telling you to let go.

3. Scaffold Partner

A scaffold **is** a vital tool upon which builders climb, helping them to lift items up, especially when it involves a high building; this makes their work fast. It is not a permanent structure on the building, but it is very vital to fast track moving kinds of stuff up. As soon as the work is completed, dry enough, and the cement/ concrete can stay on its own, the scaffold is removed. It is not part of the building at all.

Also in courtship, there are gold diggers (spiritual and physical gold diggers) who know quite well that they can never be part of that person's life in the future but are temporarily either as a spiritual gold digger and gold diggers of other virtues in your well. Note it quite well that they are dangerous.

The spiritual gold diggers are only interested in tapping your anointing and other virtues in you, thereby sapping your energy. You must take note so that you don't fall victim and, in the end, have your regret.

4.   Pillar Partner

A pillar is a solid structure on which a building rests upon and takes its strength. There is no building without support. The power of the pillar determines the longevity of the building. If there is any crack in the pillar or is not well structured, in no distant time, the building collapses. In the same vein, in courtship, a person who is likely to be a pillar in your life will show the attributes right from courtship days. How do you know this? His/her foundation in the Word of God goes a long way in sustaining yours; his/her interest in the things of God will assist you to discover your own area of weaknesses, thereby becoming both spiritual and physical pillar to support you in moving ahead.

This is the ideal partner; this type of partner is a committed partner. Commitment means staying loyal to things you said you were going to do long after the atmosphere you said it in has left you.

This is a praying partner with an enduring spirit and a functioning brain, not just handsomeness or beauty or wealthy parents. This type of partner has integrity which is doing the right thing even when no one is watching. This type of partner will always support your success. Supporting others' success won't dampen yours; it takes only a mature partner to understand this. This type of partner is one who has permitted the Holy Spirit to work in every department of his/her life. Though this person might not have all the wealth and riches in this world, there is this unexplainable inner peace and assurance you have within you. This kind of partner is teachable and will always be willing to say sorry once he/she is wrong and will not be satisfied with the explanation. This type of partner has been thoroughly broken down through the power of the Holy Spirit.

CHAPTER SIX

MISTAKES IN COURTSHIP

The Bible says the *Thought of God towards us is good not of evil to give us an expected end* (Jeremiah 29:11). God is a kind father who has programmed every good gift for his Children, including wives and husbands. Still, most often, we fail to wait on God, wait for God, or wait by God, but instead, expect God to rubber-stamp our heart desires, either such is the will of God for us or not. It was only when a wrong step had been taken, and our fingers were burnt that we realised our nonchalant attitude and ran back to God.

1.   Dwelling in the past

Most often, people find it difficult to forget their past; when they commit sin, and after praying for forgiveness, they still don't erase bad memories from their mind. Most of the time, they find it difficult to forgive themselves. This shouldn't be a typical situation with believers. It is uncalled for when such a person is a child of God that has been redeemed, broken down, spirit-filled, and his/her action is scripture-based.

There is this saying that says, "*Youth is a blunder, manhood is struggle, and old age is regret,*" which means anything done when one is not redeemed has been forgiven and written off. There is a need for total and holistic turn around spiritually and physically (restitution).

## 2.	Always talking about the things you enjoyed in past relationships

Talking about something you experienced in past relationships is not a wise thing to do. It may mean that although you are out of Egypt, Egypt is not out of you. It shows that you are still very much interested in keeping those relationships. It also could mean that you do not need the relationship you are presently into. The more you bring talk about your past relationships to your present, the more it kills love and commitment.

It is becoming a trend with the 'so-called' Christian brother or sister to always think of their past and even record regret for leaving the past for the future because of the freedom they had to commit sins before having an encounter with Christ. It should be noted that going back to one's vomit does not help spiritual growth and a heaven-bound relationship. If the current relationship is not bringing forth such things, he/she used to enjoy in the past relationship, there is the tendency of going back to his/her past, thereby breaking the courtship.

3. Comparing your past relationship to the present One

Comparing the current relationship with those that occurred in time past is unhealthy, simply because no two people can be the same, that is, individual differences are key or germane in relationships. Comparing people usually creates friction between a Lady and a Man in a relationship. Each of the parties must see the other person as a unique being that may not have all the attributes that are expected in the partner (Man or Woman). It is, therefore, essential to appreciate God's endowed characteristics in the person you are courting and not refer to the earlier relationships with past individuals.

4. Attachment to prophecies

Test all spirits and be sure of the spirit prophesying to you. This is the reason courtship and marriage are not meant for boys and girls, but for mature minds, Holy Spirit-filled, and people who befriend their Bible and know the mind of God are expected to go into courtship.

A flexible mind or immature Christian will always hold on to prophecies without verifying from God, by so doing, they make a mistake of a lifetime that can never be rectified. Your spiritual antenna must be actively connected to Jesus, once you are connected, you can never be misled. This is the reason we have to do a regular spiritual check-up to ascertain where we are in Christ. You must be in tune with the Holy spirit.

5.　Lying

Some traits are not only found among unbelieving partners but are predominating among the 'so-called! children of God. When the Bible says, "such should not be heard of amidst the elect," the Bible recorded that the devil is the father of all liars, and their part is in the lake of fire.

Anyone who deliberately lies to get what he/she want is not of God. Once you notice this act, please **flee**. Unfaithfulness also belongs to the family of lies. The Bible says, "by their fruits, you shall know them." An unfaithful brother or sister can never be stable. Unfaithfulness is a subset of lying.

7.　Deceit

Deceit is so universal, especially in the lives of lovers who are not broken down by the Holy Spirit. The devil uses this as a tool to mislead people. It is even universal nowadays that the economy does not favour getting married as it used to be in the past. Some men and ladies tend to pretend that they are more than what is feasible in them. A lady or man that is working without her spiritual eyes being opened can be easily carried away.

Some ladies hide under the canopy of being a Christian to cover up their past of several abortions, multiple relationships, and mere looking at them as pure and natural Christian without earring or makeup; you simply take them for being genuine. Watch out for the truth!

7.   Fornication

God frowns at fornication. Godly relationships should not be soiled with fornication. Eating the fruit before it is ripe is an abomination and a forbidden fruit in courtship. It should be noted that Christians should run away from everything that will bring about fornication while courting because God detests it. Some people have been married even before being eventually joined at the altar. Marriage is not when the two parties are being joined on the altar. It is the carnal knowledge of both parties that are inseparable (fornication is the carnal knowledge of both parties, which results in the mixture of fluid from both parties that unifies them to be one).

The Bible says *your body is the temple of God; anyone who defiles His temple, God himself will destroy* (I Cor 6:19). This implies that God Himself will be the supervisor of the punishment, and hence, you have no one else to turn to for deliverance in the face of His wrath.

However, the good news is that anytime you realise your wrong and show remorse and ask for forgiveness and plead for God's mercy, He is ever ready to right off your evil doings and accept you back. Isaiah 1:18 *"Come now, and let us reason together, says the Lord, though your sins are like scarlet, they shall be as white as snow; though they are red like crimson, They shall be as wool."*

CHAPTER SEVEN

PRINCIPLES IN COURTSHIP

If prayer alone can keep a home from breaking, I (Kanyinsola) think the divorced rate all across the globe should be radically reduced if not totally eliminated, which will amount to lesser home breaking apart. If giving tithes, offering, and helping others alone will make you rich and wealthy, then we should have a lower rate of poverty. But no, it's not enough. What is the implication of this statement? It means that beyond prayer, holiness, righteousness, sincerity, etc., there are things that must be done consciously and purposefully for the sake of saving and keeping your courtship from failing and falling.

Information

The reason why America is said to be the world's most powerful nation is that She have access to classified information. Information is power, knowledge is the key. The level to which you are informed is the level to which you will operate. If you want to soar, if you so wish to live a mountain top life, if you're going to rule your world, if you're going to live up to your potentials if you want to be who you are destined to be, all that you need is nothing but access to uncommon information and knowledge. The right application of your acquired information and knowledge will then become your principle.

Asides prayer and information highlighted, below are principles that we discovered in a survey we undertook with the aid of a well-structured questionnaire.

Maturity

It's not just laws birthed out of speculation but a principle birth by revelation and experience by matured married couples. By maturity, it doesn't mean to say how old they are, but how well they've been able to accept responsibilities and the implication of their decisions. We have seen lots of couples with an escapist attitude. I'm humbled to say that couples that fail to face the consequences of their choices are not matured. We took our time to interview both the old married couples and young ones, and discovered that the principle used is almost the same, though slightly different.

One of our respondents who has been married for 39 years said, "Humility is the number one principle that has helped her in falling-in-love, growing-in-love, and staying-in-love." Now, by humility, this is precisely what she means; Humility in marriage can be explained in the light of the fact that we all love to win arguments and appear as though we are the right person in any conflict; this is a very wrong attitude in marriage. Humility says one party does not see himself or herself as being superior to the other, but as helpmates and partners in the fulfilment of God's purpose in their union.

Maintain Your Attraction

Another principle is this "Keep doing what attracted your partner to you." Don't hide under the canopy of courtship with marriage in view, and then you stop doing what attracted him to you. There is always an attraction. There is the place of the will of God and spirituality; however, the fact remains that we all have one thing or the other that we desire and hope to have in our partners. These attractions and desires should be discussed by the two intending couples such that each person works on himself or herself for improvement and for continuous longing for each other.

CHAPTER EIGHT

LOVE FADES

I (Kanyinsola) was just twelve years old when I saw some marriages break apart. I saw a man beating his wife. I saw another one insulting his wife and cursing her in the presence of my friends and me. I vividly remember the look on the woman's face; she was humiliated. She barely could stand to look at our faces; she shamefully walked into her room. I was disturbed for a reason. I don't know precisely how flawless love should be, but I know that I don't want to be treated that way. I felt shocked and angry. I knew it wasn't right, and somehow something needed to be done. I kept on pondering on why a man could do such a thing to his own wife. Unknowingly I became a human rights activist to war against domestic violence and gender discrimination. I am sure the man didn't realise the magnitude of his action and the effect it had on me. I became a girl with a dream, and now I've grown to become a full fledge lady with a vision. I knew that at a stage in his life, he must have been in love with the woman. Then what happened to love? Why does it seem like love was never present? Why the hatred? My quest to get the correct answer made me carry out an interview, not just a conversation but also observation. Part of what I discovered is this; there are **moral reasons** and **spiritual reasons**.

I would start with moral reasons.

MORAL REASONS

(I.) **Expectations that are not met**: One of the parties must have thought so highly of the other person that they failed to consider the likely occurrence of the negative (unexpected). The truth is, in life, you cannot envisage what would happen in the future. The person you love so deeply that you want to build your world might not meet certain expectations in marriage. Expectations like being rich, birthing children, pampering you, giving you all his time, etc. Answer the big questions:

a.   What will you do if you eventually marry your partner, and she fails to birth a child?

b.   What if he is unable to provide all the resources you need?

c.   What if he/she becomes sick for the rest of her life or his life?

d.   What if he/she falls from the place of honour?

e.   What if that thing that attracted you to him/her fades? Would you still fulfil your promise of "Forever with you"?

Look, if you've got no answer to these questions, please take a pause long enough; do not get married yet. Be sure you have answers to these questions. It might seem like a pessimistic attitude, but they are sincere questions. I honestly think children are given to enhance your marriage. When God delays in giving you a child, you should have every reason to still remain happy in your marriage.

My sincere thoughts are these:

a.   *You need a husband/wife, not property,*

b.   *not education, not prowess, not beauty,*

c.   *not how convincingly he/she can speak,*

d.   *not his/her height, not his/her achievement,*

e.   *not anointing or how well he can preach, teach, pray or how hard he/she works,*

f.   *not his/her ideology or philosophy of life.*

g.   *not even his/her material possessions*

The truth and the undeniable truth we discovered is that all these will fade away with time (I stand to be corrected). But, a husband/wife will rise through the test of time. Husband/Wife in this context is not someone you claim to "love," not someone that you've foolishly taken a marriage vow with.

a.   It is someone who has been designed for you. It is someone who can genuinely fix that missing rib.

b.   It is someone with a divine vision for you.

c.   It is someone with a divine mandate. It is someone whose primary assignment is to work with you and on you.

A man/woman without a vision for you will bring confusion into your life. At any slight offence, the person will be gone in a twinkling of an eye, and you'll be left desolate. Before you get into marriage, you must have an attitude to do things for your spouse without expecting a reward in return. If this has become your attitude, the other person responds naturally. Check your motive, state of mind.

(ii.)   Another reason we found out is Insincerity:

Be real, be sincere, let the person love you for who you are. Don't let the person love another dimension of you entirely while the real you are kept underneath the rug. Come out of your shell. If he/she is for you, then he/she will love you with unfeigned love. Don't pretend! Pretence makes love fade out, and you might not be able to handle the result of your action. Be completely sincere. Be yourself, be you, and do you. You have no reason to be sorry for being who you are. That's your individuality and originality.

(iii.)   When you stop working on yourself:

The world is so sophisticated and competitive that you cannot afford not to improve yourself and knowledge. New technologies are emerging daily, and new styles unfolding. You must be relevant. The experience of yesterday is not enough for today's challenges. You must be teachable. You must invest heavily in your improvement and advancement - morally, academically, and spiritually. Learn daily. Keep learning.

(iv.)   When you stop doing what your spouse loves about you:

This is a great disaster. You must keep your spouse attracted to you daily. You must make that happen. If you keep doing what puts him/her off, then love automatically fades away. By doing what your spouse loves about you is simply an act of loving your spouse. You choose to do it because you love your spouse.

(v.) Pride:

You must remain humble. You must heed the advice of the right people. You mustn't think too highly of yourself. You must apologise even when you are right on a matter. It's a way of saving your courtship.

CHAPTER NINE

SPIRITUAL REASONS WHY LOVE FADES

In Chapter Eight, we shine the spotlight on the moral reasons that make Love fade. In this Chapter, we would consider the spiritual reasons that make Love Fade.

Separation from the Vine

In John 15:5 Jesus said, "I am the vine, ye are the branches: He that abideth in me, and I in him, the same bringeth forth much fruit: for without me ye can do nothing." The Major spiritual reason why love fades is separation from the vine, which is separation from Jesus. Separation from The Godhead (whose life is an exemplary display of Love, John 3:16), it is impossible to give what you do not have. For you to stay True in Love, you must have the True Love of the father in You. In Chapter Thirteen, we took a pause long enough to explain this.

Setting your Cart before your Horse

The second reason why love fades is when you "Set your cart before your horse." By this, we mean purpose before Love. Failure to understand one's purpose before getting into a relationship can be costly. As not everyone fits into God's purpose for your life. Samson didn't have a strong background in the word of God to guide the divine purpose of God jealously for him. You first must discover who you are and what God wants for you before you search for your "missing rib." If you place the former before the latter, and you discover your purpose, the person you are going out with might not fit into your God's given purpose, thereby making the love that exists between the two of you fade.

Inadequate understanding of the Word of God

Another reason why love fades is an inadequate understanding of the Bible's position on the kind of love that will lead to marriage. Emotions alone cannot sustain a relationship because emotions are not reliable. Wilful love is what sustains a marriage that Jesus displayed on the cross of Calvary. He simply submitted himself to the will of the father.

The parent also plays a significant role in ensuring that the love between the love birds remains.

I (Dr Oyeniyi) like to Consider the story of Samson and Isaac:

Parental Laxity

Samson was a bountiful gift given by God to his parents and was a Nazarene from conception, which suggests that he would be a servant of God. Still, unfortunately, Samson was not tutored adequately by his parents. It wasn't recorded that his parents told him of the encounter they had before his birth and the instruction given by God to the Israelites not to marry from a strange land. He engaged in a relationship that paved the way for his untimely death. Hence, the result of Parental Laxity.

Negligence to Parental Counsel

The Bible says spare the rod and spoils the child (proverb 13:24). Samson was always allowed to have his way. It is a common mistake that parents make; parents should tailor the lives of their children in the way of God. He didn't listen to his parent's counsel on who to marry, unlike Isaac, who was also the only child of his parents but followed their instructions to the letter. Here, we are not just referring to your biological parents, it could be your spiritual parents. Understand these sets of people's experiences so that you can tap from them.

Self Sufficiency

Not under spiritual leader(s) and not accountable to any spiritual authority in your local assembly or fellowship who would teach the ways of the Lord to you that will help fine-tune your spirit together and make you grow together. This is incumbent for your belief to be Bible-based. Absence of this could cause your love to fade as various teachings negate the Bible's stand on love.

It is imperative to be accountable to a spiritual leader whom God will use to reprove and correct you from time to time.

CHAPTER TEN

COMMON MISTAKES

Mistakes are actions or decisions that are wrong or produce results that are not correct or not intended. Mistakes could be in many aspects, e.g., career, association, daily dealing, etc. Some errors may be healthy, while some are costly. While it is true that some mistakes will make you smarter, better, and more intelligent, on the other hand, some errors pose a threat to your future and could bring all of your aspirations, goodwill, and vision to naught. There are thousands of reasons people make mistakes; below are the common mistakes.

1.   Doing the right thing at the wrong time makes the right thing wrong

Although the Bible says that it is not suitable for the man to be alone, I will make a help meet for him. But it is a mistake to go into courtship when God has not approved it nor given you the go-ahead to do so. It is merely a waste of time. Wasting time is to do the right thing at the wrong time. Not all items that are seemingly good should be involved in. Doing the right thing at the wrong time makes it wrong. Doing the wrong thing at the right time is makes it wrong. Be guided; Time is life!

The decision to go into courtship is not what you should do under duress. You need to be like the men of Issachar who understood signs of times. Some things may be morally right, culturally right, and socially acceptable but are spiritually wrong! It is a complete waste of time to do something God has not told you to do. We encourage you to wait for a release from God before going into courtship so you won't be wasting your precious time. If you keep rushing and running ahead of God, God will be compelled to wait for you to exhaust your schemes.

If you really want to get it right, you need to be patient. You must not be anxious. Trust in the **LORD** with all your heart and lean not unto thy own understanding.

My Ordeal (Kanyinsola): One of the mistakes I made was that I did not rest in the Lord and in his ability to help me. I felt that the next thing for my life after completing my B.Sc. was to get married. I wasn't patient enough to hear Him properly before entering into the relationship I recently broke from, Glory to God for His revelation, and His prompting to break the bond. Now, I am happy and fulfilled.

My advice is for you to wait on the Lord, wait patiently for Him. Don't keep doing trial and error; don't keep running up and down. He never comes late, and whatever He does is at the right time. His thought for you is for good and not for evil to give you an expected end. Don't act until God has acted.

2. Eagerness and Anxiety to Have a Taste of Relationship

This is an ungodly prompting. Do not be eager or anxious to be in a relationship. Once the devil notices any form of eagerness in you, he may bring deceit your way. This deceit will affect your dreams and influence the things you hear.

Each time you are eager to do something, it means you are telling God to stay out of the situation. You are becoming like Prophet Balaam, who twisted the hand of God to get what he wanted, and God let him go into destruction.

You must understand that nothing will be right if it is not in God's time for you. Nothing will be appropriate if you do it ahead of God's time. The fact that you have graduated from University, you've also completed your M.Sc. / MBA /Ph.D., as the case may be, doesn't mean marriage is the next thing God has for you. Of course, it's one of His intentions, plans, and will for you. Each individual has a different pattern for their lives; the same way our fingerprints differ, God's thoughts, ideas, and purpose for us for each one of us also changes. It is, therefore, important for you to wait on God's divine timing for your life.

3.   Trying to Play God

Most youths try to play God in choosing their life partner. This should not be so. Deuteronomy 29:29 says, "The *secret things belong unto the Lord our God, but those things which are revealed belong unto us and to our children forever that we may do all the words of this law.*" It is one thing to pray, it is another thing to wait to hear God's instructions. Some people are too impatient and are misled into running after fortune-tellers: God's will and ways past finding out by anybody.

Let's liken prayer to a farmer who sows seeds for harvest. A farmer is a patient man who sows his seed in the ground and then goes on his way, sleeping and waking up. Eventually, the field brings forth its own yield. The farmer does not know how the harvest will come or exactly when it will come, but his job is to get up in the morning, till the ground, and go to sleep at night.

A farmer never knows precisely when his crops will come in, but he does what he can do to enrich the soil and cultivate his crops but leaves the rest in the hands of the creator. After you must have prayed, fasted, and attended marriage seminars of all sorts, you must wait on God to play His part by directing you. You cannot force God to speak; He speaks when He is ready to talk. Don't start doing random sampling, so you don't give the food meant for the children to the dog.

Wait patiently with the right attitude, for there is no harm in waiting. Instead, some youths wait for the fullness of time and continue working on their spirituality, morality, potentiality, academics, and other areas of their life that need improvement. Do not be as the heathen that keeps running after shadows; no one ever catches shadows.

The reason God might not have spoken to some people about their life partner might be that He still wants them to take some bad habits away, break away from some beliefs, and develop the right attitudes. The most important thing is that, while waiting, you must not waste away. Don't just be looking around for whom to marry; work on yourself. While waiting, you must be productive.

4.   Pressure from Within and Without

This pressure is an ungodly prompting that makes people run ahead of God and eventually miss it martially. Yes, trouble abounds—pressure from parents, friends, colleagues, sexual urge, environment, etc. The pressure is normal, but the strange thing will be for you to let it push you into Courtship when it is not yet time. Do not listen to the voice of pressure. You will definitely get someone to marry at God's appointed time. Slow and steady wins the race. You must be patient enough and must be able to identify the voice of God and the voice of pressure. A person who follows pressure from within and without reaps typically destruction. I've seen it several times. If you ever fret into a relationship, you will be frightened out.

CHAPTER ELEVEN

INGREDIENTS IN COURTSHIP

Here in Africa, we have a delicacy called Jollof Rice and the local one called Concoction Rice. There are ingredients and recipes for preparing Jollof rice, and if you miss out on one of the ingredients, the rice might look like Jollof Rice but will not taste like it. It will be concoction Rice (Nigeria's less glamorous style of making Jollof rice). Also, in courtship, some ingredients must be carefully applied if you must enjoy and not endure Courtship. Also, if it must produce the exact picture, God has in mind for instituting it. Here are some of the ingredients (Diligence and Information), apply them into your courtship, and you will be amazed by the result.

Diligence:

Diligence is the conscientiousness or determination or perseverance when doing something. There is no such thing as a perfect partner. The Word, "perfection" is not evidential in human nature. We have been wrongly taught that if a person is Born Again and Holy Ghost filled, the person will be flawless. No! This is not true. Unknowingly, a person might hurt you or say things that disgust you, not because it is deliberate or intentional. It is a manifestation of our human trait/nature.

Gold, in its original or raw form, looks so unpleasant and unattractive, but the moment it passes through all the refinement process, it then becomes brighter, attractive, and beautiful. Also, is everyone. Never write off a man or woman whose character is terrible or whose perception about life is different from yours. You never can tell what they will become once they have access to the information that transformed your life. A newly conceived baby is not expected to remain a baby for life. The babyhood is for a stipulated time. Steadily but gradually, they grow from a day old to a month old. Progressively they begin to learn to sit, smile, laugh, crawl, learn to pronounce their first Word, and before you realise it, the baby has become a grown man/woman. I must not fail to mention this; somethings, we probably didn't notice what happened.

First, the mother must have fed the child with the right food that contains essential nutrients that will aid the growth of the child (in this context, it means healthy information that has shaped the baby), so it is with the human. The fact that someone does something poorly is not enough reason to give up on them (except they are not ready to improve and do not allow for a healthy change).

Concerning this context, you might not get a complete/finished man/woman. If he/she is perfect in the literal sense, then, there will be no space for you. It means he/she has all that he needs to be who God wants him/her to be. It's a two-way flow. You rub off on your partner, and your partner will rub off on you. Courtship is not supposed to be a one-way flow or a parasitic relationship, it should be a symbiotic flow. For God to have permitted the coming together of both of you, it means there is a vacuum that you must fill. And sometimes, it means you might have to first clean up that vacuum, bring out the dirt, and trust me, it's going to cost you something. That something is what I'm going to bring to your notice.

Seldom do we take our time to understand the principle of influencing a person for a positive and productive change. You must know that before you came into the person's life, certain things were in place. You must also understand that they derive joy from different things, and those things have influenced their mindset, belief system, and ideology. Your ability to understand this truth will go a long way to ensuring you make the best out of your relationship. Never believe the lie of changing/ influencing someone in a short while. Even if they seem to have changed, the changes could be temporary; probably, they just got caught in the in-love obsession, or maybe they let their emotions get the best of them for that moment.

For instance, a Twenty – Five (25) year old lady must have adopted and developed principles and philosophy over time. It's impossible to bring about a sudden change in just six months of your courtship with her. Some changes could occur in a short while, but most of the other things would take a longer time to be erased or influenced. It is in this realisation most people falter. No patience, no persistence, no prayer, no communion, and the lady/gentleman just jumped into a relationship nations are to benefit from. You must understand that the birth of something valuable does not come on a platter of gold.

I (Dr Oyeniyi) have seen the reward of Diligence in relationships over time. I have had the opportunity of interviewing couples, trust me, they don't look like their past mistakes, wrong principles, philosophy, and belief. They are better, brighter, attractive, beautiful, spiritual, intelligent, and successful than they were at the initial stage – when they were in their raw form. But by merely persevering, their relationship has become healthy. One of the significant reasons courtship fails (though not limited to the reason(s) here) is because of lack of diligence. Although it looks like an audacious statement, I beg your pardon if it offends you. Diligence is the quality of being strategic, resilient, and enduring.

Persistence is the conscientiousness or determination or perseverance when hoping to achieve something. See the keyword **"Conscientiousness"** – that means your will, emotion, and mind is involved; you are fully aware and aiming at a goal. Diligence includes hard work, spirituality, and confession of positive words alone cannot replace or take the place of persistence. If prayer alone is enough to make the relationship work, I think most relationships will not fail.

There is a place of prayer, and there is a place of labour. You must invest in materials that will improve your capacity; you must be willing to break away from unhealthy stereotypes and deliberate decisions to make things work. There is no replacement for hard work; hard work in praying together, studying the Word of God together, investing in the life-transforming book, attending marriage seminars and conferences, etc. The difference has always been information. Knowledge is light, and ignorance is darkness. Invest time in encouraging your partner and affirming your unconditional love to him/her. Diligence is not just hard work; but strategic positioning. It involves the sacrifice of your time, energy, and resources.

The revelation of Christ as being loving must find expression in you, not just in the spirit and faith but also in your relationship. If your relationship is not working and you are sure you have received conviction from the Holy Spirit about your partner, many times, the problem is not from God, check your receptive system, check your mindset, check yourself. It may be that you are missing something. Outstanding success in courtship comes with a massive price out of which diligence is one. Do not doubt God's Word. Late Tai Solarin (The Founder of May Flower school) wrote, and I quote, "We shall work even if we must work our fingers to the bone, so may it be!

CHAPTER TWELVE

COURTSHIP: THE MISSED DART

Having the right understanding of relationships, especially in courtship, is germane if it must lead to walking to the Altar together. You should shed off the lust in your heart and approach courtship in light of God's purpose for it. If one party is beclouded at the initial stage of courtship, then the purpose of going into it might be lost. Some people have been victims of not counting their costs, they allow sentiment to rule their minds. Hence, they miss their focus, thereby leading to making mistakes.

Sex:

Marriage is not an end to your problems, especially if you have a sexual problem. Marriage is not all about sex, though it's one of the reasons. Sex is a deep relationship between a man and a woman; it involves the union of the sexual organ. It is the penetration of the female organ by the male organ. However, it should be noted that Sex is not from the devil; it is from God; the devil didn't create it, God did. So, Sex is not carnality. Not obeying divine precept on Sex is carnality, and it has destroyed destinies; because in Sex, life is being poured into another life.

Marriage is not a cure for sexual sin. David was married, yet, he fell into sexual immorality; the same was the case of Abraham and Potiphar's wife (she told Joseph, lay with me). Sexual temptation increases when you get married, your sexual drive increases. The issue of sex is not going to stop because you are married. The Bible noted it clearly that sex must be done between a husband and a wife, not between a brother and a sister (still in the courting process not yet married). There are so many problems you have, that marriage will not solve. Please, don't get me wrong! Understand exactly what I(Dr Oyeniyi) mean. In fact, when you marry, your problems also marry themselves confirming the scripture that says two shall be one.

Loneliness:

Don't get married because you are tired of being alone. You can be married and still be lonely. Loneliness is, therefore, a state of mind. Marriage is not a cure to your "loneliness"; if it were a cure, why then did Adam go his way and left his wife behind, and the serpent beguiled her? Because he didn't see his divine purpose as to why God brought Eve into his life.

Need:

Don't get married because you want someone to assist you financially if you do, you may regret the outcome. Marriage is not for lazy individuals. In fact, you might be more frustrated financially when married because you will have more responsibilities to shoulder, you will no longer look out for yourself alone. Still, you will have to look out for your wife/husband, children, mother-in-law/ father-in-law, etc.

Pastoral Instruction:

Don't get married because your pastor said it is God's will for you. Be thoroughly convinced. You are the one getting married, not the man/woman of God. It is your life that will be positively or negatively affected, not the life of the man of God.

Fear of Being Jilted:

Some marry because they have been jilted, and because they do not want to be jilted again, they do everything possible to avoid being jilted. Look, whosoever loves you will never leave you for someone else. The African proverb says that "the water someone will drink will never flow past the person." In the process of avoiding being jilted, you might fall into the wrong hand, and the person you get married to could be a thorn in your flesh. Never be in a hurry for any reason whatsoever. "Desperation and obsession about someone as a single person may just be a sign that you are not supposed to marry them." The fruit of righteousness is always peace, quietness, and confidence. The moment you begin to feel you will die if you don't get them, then you shouldn't. This was a statement Nathaniel Bassey (a Nigerian-based gospel singer) posted on his Instagram page sometimes ago.

Marriage is not all about now; it is about later. The man or woman you see now may not be the same man or woman he/she would be in the next 15-30 years. If Marriage is all about now, why do people who started well – based on what they call love – end up becoming enemies? Why does the sister who was initially fervent when you met her become someone who doesn't even like to hear about God? You need to pray and pray through. You need to ask God to reveal who he or she is, who he or she will become in the future, and the assignment given to him/her by God, and then, see whether you are compatible or not. The person you see now may just be a shadow or a mist that will soon disappear.

Marriage is more in-depth than what you see; you only see things on the surface. There are lots of unforeseen challenges that await one in marriage, and that is why it is good you get married when you have discovered God's will for your life martially, and you are sure of it.

If you are in a relationship and you are not sure it is where God wants you to be, or you don't have peace (I mean inner peace), I advise you to quit and go and pray more.

While some people's testimony about marriage, maybe "marriage is good," the evidence of others possibly is "had I known." The difference may be that some people might be patient enough to wait on God and follow His leadings; others may not wait upon God for direction. The Bible says to cast your cares upon him for he cares for you. If you do not throw your concerns upon him, then, don't blame him when things go ill for you in your marriage. God is a perfect gentle father, He will not force you to trust Him; but if you do His will, you will be glad you did. For your joy will be unspeakable!

The marital journey is not the kind one must endure; it is a journey you must enjoy because that's how God created and destined it to be. Even if you are faced with particular challenges, you will still be joyful because the Lord is the One who led you into it, and you shall not want (Psalm 23:1); your victory is certain.

CHAPTER THIRTEEN

THINGS TO DO DURING COURTSHIP

In this Chapter, we articulate our suggestions on what should be done in courtship. The saying doing the right thing at the right time and in the right circumstance will make our lives be as smart darts that strikes at places that matter has proven to be true over the years. Here are guidelines on what you should do in case you are clueless about what to do and how to love your spouse more intelligently.

Love your Partner:

Courtship is the time to love your partner genuinely; this is the number one thing you must do. This is the foundation on which the other structure is built. When your partner errs, it will be easy to forgive him/her because of the love that exists between the two of you. Where love abounds, joy abounds too. You definitely will be able to care for and remember your partner in prayers because of the love that exists in your heart for him/her.

Study your Partner:

Also, courtship is the time to study your partner, understand his/her behaviour, and know your partner's likes and dislikes. Courtship is a time to disagree for you to agree with your partner without the intervention of any third party.

Agreement

Courtship is the period to agree on purpose and design ways to solve possible problems that might emerge in the future. Courtship is the period of asking intelligent questions; it is a time for clarification. Courtship is the time to know about your family backgrounds.

And

- Courtship is the period of understanding your partner's love language; understand why your partner behaves in a certain way.
- It is not the time to sweep any issue under the carpet. It is the time to reveal your past mistakes and errors
- Courtship is the time to wash your dirty linens before each other. It is time to love intelligently, not blindly.
- Courtship is the time to work on yourself and develop your potential.

- Courtship is the time to become competent and pillar friends. It is time to be intentional in friendship.

CHAPTER FOURTEEN

STEER CLEAR

In courtship, the parties involved should take note and understand that they are yet to be transported into the real deal called **Marriage**. You should not begin to cohabit during this period. This is not the time for them to start to wear the same clothes. This is not the time to have a joint account because they are not yet married. You should not begin to bear the same name at this stage. You should not be too close or intimate as married couples do. You should not start hugging, kissing, romancing, caressing, touching, and smooching themselves. If you do, the implication is that you are merely setting the horse before the cart. I'm sure you know the end result. Collision and destruction **Note:** you are not married until you are married.

Courtship is the time to love intelligently; though you are in love, you are not blind. It is the time to question the question; it's not the time to close one's eyes to attitudes/behaviours that can create problems that would lead to separation when you finally get married. It is the time to take heed, seek godly counsel, be smart, and above all, watch and pray.

Courtship is not the time to visit each other in dark places or secluded corners, as this can easily cause your fall into sexual temptations; you have to beware lest you eat the forbidden fruit. It is time to create strategies on how to develop your potential, career, and life goals.

Courtship is the time to paint a clear picture of the type of home and family you desire to build and have. It is the time to begin to commit your home into the hand of God. Courtship is the time to continually develop your spirituality. It is not the time to keep secrets. Be open to yourself, be opened to God, be opened to your godly counsellors, and be opened to your godly parents. Do not keep secrets at this stage. Courtship is not the time for intercourse, A wrong step in Courtship can wreck the destinies of the partners. Courtship is not the time to assume. Ask questions, take time to dig deep. Take time to retreat and pray well, pray to God to reveal secret things you need to know about your partner. Courtship is also a time to pray, eye-opening prayers. God will open your eyes to see the future and the possible problems that might come your way; it is time to equip yourself for the journey ahead. Equip yourself spiritually, mentally, emotionally, materially, and other **LLY** you will need.

Elisha prayed a wrong prayer; he prayed that God should kill him. Instead, God sent his Angel to feed him, and he (Elisha) ran in the strength of the food the Angel of God supplied him with for 40 days. Courtship is the time to wait upon God to feed you with the food you need to strengthen you, so you will be able to run the race set before you.

Courtship is a time to do proper checks and balances. You really have to be sincere in doing this. Ask yourself serious questions that will move you forward and develop you. Questions like these:

- Am I really broken?
- Have I indeed allowed God to work freely in me?
- Am I lazy?
- Do I have an anger problem?
- Do I take my time to understand people?
- Am I sacrificial?
- Can I go out of my way to help my partner and others?
- Am I self-centred?
- Do I really care about others?
- Am I hostile?
- Am I accommodating?
- Am I emotionally stable and mature?
- When people despise, reject, and neglect me, how do I react?
- Do I flare up at any little provocation?
- How well do I table my grievances?
- Am I proud?

Courtship is a time to ask serious questions of this sort and work on them intentionally and prayerfully. If you don't seem to get the desired result, set your fiancé/fiancée as a watch over you. This is a time you need to be more teach-able for you to be divinely accessible. The bad attitudes and behaviours you refuse to stop would eventually affect your home.

Courtship is the time to discover God's will for your home and begin to walk in line with His purpose. Courtship is the time to love your partner the right way. Talking of love, what so many people consider as love is really not love? It is merely lust! Love is an act of leaving your way to help the other, it is an act of sacrificing and letting go of your personal creed. It is simply unselfish devotion.

Jesus came to the world because He loves us (John 3:16). In the process of displaying and revealing his love for us, he did two things:

1.   He gave Himself for us (Unconditional Love)

2.   He died for us (Sacrificial Love)

If you claim to love your fiancé/fiancée and all you do is to sleep with him/her, let me politely tell you that what you have towards him/her is nothing but lust. If you truly love him/her, you will not encourage any sinful act against his/her body and God.

The Bible says *your body is the temple of God, and anyone who defiles His temple, God Himself will destroy* (I Corinthians 6:19). If you genuinely love your partner, you will not assist the devil in bringing down the wrath of God upon your partner. Of all sins, God Himself will supervise the punishment of premarital Sex.

I Cor13: 4 – 7 Explain deeply what love really means, let's look at it.

Verse 4: "*Charity suffereth long and is kind; charity envieth not; charity vaunteth, not itself, is not puffed up.*"

Verse 5: "*Doth does not behave itself unseemly, seeketh not her own, is not easily provoked, **thinketh no evil.***"

Verse 6: "*Rejoiceth not in iniquity, but rejoiceth in the truth;*"

Verse 7: "*Beareth all things, believeth all things, hopeth all things, endureth all things.*"

This verse of the Bible has fully explained everything that love entails. Anything different from this is nothing but evil. Recently, a friend (Moyinoluwa) sent me (Kanyinsola) a confession he has carefully carved out of 1Cor: 13: 4–8 using The Passion translation version, and I found it helpful. I shared it with a couple of people, and the testimony is incredible.

Every morning endeavour to say the words patiently

"I am large and incredibly patient

I am gentle and consistently kind to all

I refuse to be jealous when blessing comes to someone else

I do not brag about my achievements nor inflate my own importance.

I do not dwell in shame and disrespect,

Nor selfishly seek my own honour,

I am not easily irritated or quick to take offence.

I joyfully celebrate honesty and find no delight in what is wrong

I am a safe place of shelter, for I never stop believing the best for others

I never take failure as defeat, for I never give up

I never stop loving.

You must understand that the most important tool the devil uses to fragment lives and destinies is Sex. A fragmented life will find it challenging to be focused; such a life will find it challenging to stick to a partner (if they eventually marry); it births emotional trauma, negative thinking, and soul ties.

Anything that is not the truth is simply not the truth. The truth is one and has no other version. Christ said I am the way, the truth, and the life. Any love outside the truth is likened unto this in the Bible, "*But he that heareth, and doeth not, is like a man that without foundation built a house upon the earth, against which the stream did beat vehemently, and immediately it fell, and the ruin of that house was great.*" (Luke 6:49). The reason the house fell was that it had no foundation; hence, the storms of life, and as time turned the page, it affected the building and brought it down.

Let me (Kanyinsola) ask you a question: supposing you went to the market to buy salt, and you added the right quantity of the salt into the food you are cooking. You tasted it, and it was tasteless? You further added the whole of the remaining salt, but it was still tasteless, what would you do? Luke 14:34 -35, don't be a tasteless salt by rebelling against the will and dictates of God.

CHAPTER FIFTEEN

CONSEQUENCES

Courtship is meant to be enjoyed primarily when it exists between two lovers who are friends. Real friends will be careful not to offend the other or even talk of breaking up. *'Can two people walk together except they agree'* (Amos 3:3). The binding cord in Courtship is true love and the ability to stay together in faithfulness with understanding it requires. Children of God who are in love must base their Courtship on the Word of God. The relationship must be divinely managed in order not to fall victim of the devil. Human beings have a similar nature, but the difference between the children of God is **"Christ."** A house that has its foundation upon the rock cannot crumble. This is the reason Christian courtship is different from the one practised among unbelievers.

1.   Sex in Courtship

Certain norms are taken to be healthy in the Courtship of the unbelievers, such as staying together in an enclosure that can give room for sin. The devil is smart and cunning to suggest touching, kissing, and body contact, which will eventually lead to carnal knowledge of each other. Before one realizes it, sin is committed.

This suffices that the two have allowed little foxes to spoil their vines. The foundation of the home to be built has been placed on the everlasting curse. There is no other name to call it than fornication, which God frowns at. The fear of the Lord is the beginning of wisdom; a partner, husband or wife-to-be who does not detest whatever grieves the Holy Spirit will not see anything wrong in breaking your heart as a husband or wife.

The Courtship that does not compromise Christian principles will surely precede to a happy Christian family, knowing full well that 'by humility and the fear of God are riches, and honour and life.' We have no other way of living except by the Word. It should be noted that tests, trials, and temptations are not meant for animals but for human beings. Temptations will come, one way or the other, and when they arrive, the only force to counter and overcome them is the Word of God. No wonder the Bible says, "*Flee from all appearances of the Evil*" (I Thessalonians 5:22-24); whatever you do not like to eat, there is no need to smell it.

2.   Believing in one's Strength

The Bible records that *by strength shall no man prevail.* (I Samuel 2:9b). Some Christians believe so much in themselves and their level of spirituality; they think they cannot fall to temptation. This may look funny because the devil has no business than to tempt the beloved. If the Lord Jesus Christ was not big enough for the devil to tempt, how much more Christians who keep praying for forgiveness of sins daily? If we can depend on our spirituality, the Bible would not have stated that we should flee!

We should not forget that the reason for going into a relationship differs. Deceit may set in just because of certain qualities found in one, and to discern such will require God's guidance and leading of the Holy Spirit. Cases are rampant where strangers go to the church in search of suitable materials for wives after having lived a wayward life and vice versa. A person's spiritual strength may not be enough to detect hence the need to seek the face of God and the right counsel from fervent children of God.

It will not be an overstatement that some ministers or in some ministries, they match-make brothers and sisters for Marriage because they do not want their members to marry from other denominations. Such people who trust in Pastors, leaving God out, later discover that they are not fit for each other; it eventually becomes eternal sorrow or may even lead to loss of lives. This suggests that you should court a partner that you love, and someone fit to be your friend and brother and vice-versa.

3.   Oath Taking

The Bible says, 'for this reason shall a man leave his father and his mother and shall cleave to his wife.' Man is ordained by God to marry; this means that a mature, strong, and hardworking man is qualified to marry, not a boy. Someone who understands and is ready to be responsible for his actions can marry.

What we see nowadays are lovers making oaths and even going to the level of involving covenants! A vow is taken only during the wedding to seal the union. Ignorantly, some Christians make vows to their fiancée/fiancé even before going to the altar to ascertain their sincerity of purpose, forgetting that unforeseen circumstances may be a barrier in getting married at the end. Such vows at times stand against future achievements. It is ungodly to make a promise(s) that will not be fulfilled at the end, more so that the Word of God says, 'let your nay be nay, and your yea is yea.'

Our God is Holy, and everyone that will worship Him must worship Him in spirit and in truth. Some actions which should have been avoided if abhorred or kept as secret may eventually stand against getting to our destination. We need to understand the fact that we cannot put gold on a bad foundation, it will not blend. The foundation of a Christian home requires the wisdom of God and the solid Word of God to stand the test of time.

4.   Too much visitation

It is natural that as lovers, the yearning to see each other every day is very high, not for anything but to just talk and discuss at length. However, at the end of the day, ask what the discussion is all about, there is no reasonable thing discussed.

As children of God, visitation during courtship should not be too frequent in order not to err. When it is quite necessary to visit, it should be at a neutral place where both will sit down to probe issues that will affect their future positively. Both partners should try and discover their areas of weaknesses spiritually and how to assist themselves in having a consolidated family of God.

It is necessary to know that marriage is not just for fun but a serious matter which God himself ordained; He is interested in it, and it must be handled with all the seriousness it deserves. Prayer is the key that opens all doors. A prayerless Christian is a powerless one. If your prayer life is weak or not even there at all, it will be discovered early enough in courtship, and help can be sought. The visitation of Christian lovers during Courtship is meant to develop them spiritually and physically, for the purpose of marriage.

Visitations during courtship should be meaningful. It should be a time to discuss pertinent issues that will assist both partners in moving on as they progress into marriage.

5.   Compatibility

Most Christians find it difficult to critically examine and take care of this aspect before getting married. We should pause a little here; surely, God is sovereign, He has all the power to move mountains, but then He is the owner of wisdom which He has given to man to manage challenges of life. Problems can emanate if an **AS** marries an **AS** and gives birth to a Sickle cell (SS) child. The parent will always be in the agony of whether the child will live or die, aside from the psychological trauma on the family members and severe pains that the child will always go through.

The gift of medical knowledge is from God Himself, and it must be wisely utilized to assist us in living a comfortable and pain-free life. Hence, the need for lovers to go through blood Group tests, Genotype and HIV. Neglecting this aspect is like postponing the evil days, which may be more traumatic than can be imagined. A broken relationship is better than a broken marriage.

6.   Information on pertinent issues

Being beautiful or handsome is not a yardstick for a successful future marriage. Some key points are vital to be discussed if marriage is to stand the test of time. Both partners should know each person's likes and dislikes, family background, parent disposition to the relationship, living with family members, financial management, number of children to settle for, having children of different sexes in Marriage, if there is a delay in childbearing how to manage it, does the age gap really mean anything, areas of interest and others as may be applicable.

Civilization has opened our eyes to a lot of things that can be positively adopted to assist in the relationship. Gone were the days when parents give out their children in marriage without the consent of the person concerned. Life can be better when things are put in proper places, and we are cognizant of those things that interfere negatively in our wellbeing. 'A stitch in time saves nine.'

All these are mistakes you must avoid in your courtship. Some mistakes are healthy, while some are costly; avoid making costly mistakes because of its eternal consequences and the scar of which might remain forever.

However, the above-listed errors are not the only mistakes singles make in the choice of selecting life patterns. It is not limited to the mistakes as mentioned earlier.

CHAPTER SIXTEEN

KNOWING GOD'S WILL IN MARRIAGE

We are aware that part of our readers might be singles who aren't in a relationship (dating or courtship). We feel the need to provide insights on how to identify the will of God in marriage. Lots of persons think of identifying the will of God to be one who has the same passion you have for God, someone who is fervent, someone whose experience is not far from yours. In contrast, some think of someone whom you attend the same denomination. We strongly believe those recommendations are helping you set the cart before the horse. Some think of it as the person you see in your visions, dreams, someone who coincidentally spoke the same thing you heard in your spirit. All this could lead to a dead-end!

Knowing the will of God is one of the easiest things God does for his children. It doesn't come with much difficulty. While some people might not have a leading as to what God wants from them, it might be a way of God telling you to exercise patience. Some are driven by fear of settling with the wrong person.

We like to emphasize that "**marriage is not about now. The person you see today might not be the same in the next five years.**" Just as you aren't the same person, you were years back. Some factors are responsible for your changes now.

In the Dealings of Jesus with men, where he blessed the loaves of bread and thousands eat from it, it was recorded on two occasions, one thing caught my attention, shall we Look into the Bible?

Matthew 15: 32

Then Jesus called his disciples unto him and said, I have compassion on the multitude, because they continue with me now three days, and have nothing to eat: and I will not send them away fasting, lest they faint in the way.

33:   And his disciples say unto him, whence should we have so much bread in the wilderness, as to fill so great a multitude?

34: And Jesus saith unto them, how many loaves have ye? And they said, Seven, and a few little fishes

*35: And he commanded the multitude to **sit** down on the ground.*

In two instances, he commanded them to sit. We interpreted it to mean they must have been standing in anticipation to see what he would do for them. Thereby causing their (Soul, Body, Spirit) to be eager. Of a truth, it is not outrightly wrong to want to see what will come forth, but Jesus gave them a clear instruction to Sit! We submit to you today that the first thing to do in knowing the will of God is for you to Sit. You need to be in a state of total dependence on God. state of rest (allowing your body to be still) Not being agitated Not being anxious

Psalm 110: 1 "A Psalm of David. The LORD said unto my Lord, sit thou at my right hand until I make thine enemies thy footstool."

1 Kings 19:11-12 New International Version (NIV)

[11] The LORD said, "Go out and stand on the mountain in the presence of the LORD, for the LORD is about to pass by. Then a great and powerful wind tore the mountains apart and shattered the rocks before the LORD, but the LORD was not in the wind. After the wind, there was an earthquake, but the LORD was not in the earthquake. [12] After the earthquake came a fire, but the LORD was not in the fire. And after the fire came a gentle whisper."

One would have thought God would speak out while it quaked, and in the fire, but no, he spoke in a gentle whisper. To hear clearly from the Lord without mistaking the voice of your Emotions, passion, and like, your mind must be still. *Psalm 4 verse 4 "Stand in Awe, and sin not: commune with your own heart upon your bed and be still. God speaks in stillness.*

The first thing we suggest is that you must be at rest. Your mind must be at rest. You must trust him completely. His Words say the thoughts I have for you are of Good and not of evil to give you an expected end. If your creator (God) has said this about you, why shouldn't you be at rest in him?

Be rest assured that he has you secured in his arm. In due season would direct and lead you. By the statement "be at rest," we do not mean to be nonchalant. You need to be concerned about your marital life, but not worried. What is the difference between concern and worry? Let me illustrate. Every time I cross the traffic-jammed street of Lagos, I am concerned about what I am doing – but not worried.

Concern means realizing what the challenges are and calmly taking steps to meet them while worrying means going around in a maddening, futile circle. Running at a frantic pace without getting nowhere.

Also, we strongly advise you not to allow fear into your mind. Fear of settling down late. Fear of not marrying the wrong person and other fears you might think about. The moment you are afraid, you have prepared a feast for the unclean spirit. The devil definitely would want to prey on such a mind. "2 Timothy 1:7 For God hath not given us the spirit of fear; but of power, and of love, and of a sound mind."

Besides, we also would not hesitate to mention here that you must learn to meditate. This is one of the potent ways God directs and speaks to us his Children. Genesis 24: 63, "And Isaac went out to meditate in the field at the eventide: and he lifted up his eyes, and saw, and, behold, the camels were coming." Isaac went out to take advantage of the silent evening, and a single field, for meditation and prayer. While he was meditating, he saw Rebecca on the camels. Each time we engage ourselves in meditation, we create a free and open prospect of the heavens above us, and the earth around us, and the hosts and riches of both, by the view of which we should be led to the contemplation of the Maker and Owner of all. The channel of our spirit will be open to hearing from God and to our receptive system would be open to receive inspiration from God on what to do and whom he has prepared for you. It is probable Isaac was now praying for good success in the affair of his marriage and meditating upon that which was proper to encourage his hope in God concerning it. Now, when he sets himself, as it were, upon his watchtower, to see what God would answer him, he sees the camels coming. Meditation is not aimless thinking or mundane thinking. It is a channel of communicating with God in our spirit.

The Fourth point is to keep praying for the perfect will of God. In line with this, do not be carried away by numerous visions, dreams, and revelation. Subject it to time. Let the word of God guide you through.

The antidote to not making mistakes is wisdom. A life void of wisdom is bound to make regrettable errors and mistakes. Wisdom is key. It is paramount. A life void of wisdom is bound to make repeated mistakes. A Chinese proverb says, "Cheat me once, you are a fool, Cheat me twice, I am a fool." This suffices to mean that if you allow yourself to be cheated twice, that repeating the same mistakes over again, it means wisdom is unavoidable absent in such life. The wisdom in this context denotes the kind of wisdom that only God gives. It is not the heathen kind of wisdom. The Bible makes it clear in 1 Corinthians 1:25 makes it clear that *the foolishness of God is wiser than man's wisdom, and the weakness of God is stronger than man's strength.*

Upon the application of those suggestions listed, be patient. The Holy Spirit in you will unfold the plans of God as you walk in faith with him.

EPILOGUE

You have finished this book. What have you read? Simply a series of common mistakes in Christian courtship, series practical and workable suggestions for a healthy courtship.

This book was birth by the desire to help you avoid making mistakes in your courtship. Courtship is peculiar to the parties involved, how your courtship will be, is solely dependent on you and your partner. Just as it is wrong to administer the same treatment for a cancerous patient to a patient with malaria. It will be wrong if we fail to tell you the truth. What works in my (Dr Aderonke) situation might not work in yours because of the peculiarity of my case. How I met my husband (HRM Oba Dr Adetoyese Oyeniyi) will not be the same as yours. The challenges I experience might not be the exact one you will face, hence, the need to be subject to the leadings of the Holy Spirit.

What we have patiently articulated in this book are guidelines on Ideal Christian Courtship. While some species of Christian believe it is wrong for the intending couple to visit themselves, some believe it is right while some are neutral about it. The dealings in your courtship solely depend on your emotional maturity, spiritual understanding, moral upbringing, among other factors. The causative factor leading to dissolving courtship defers. The same factor that led to dissolving a courtship could be the reason why another courtship is well united. It depends on how those issues are handled. Disagreement should not be lightly treated. While some disagreements can ruin an evening, others have the capacity to ruin a promising relationship.

What we have highlighted in the chapters You've read, we think, should help you identify what works for you. We have also provided you with the principle to follow to arrive at a solution to the challenges your courtship may pose to you.

A real child of God must never stop repenting. By this, we mean he or she should take responsibility for his or her actions and ask God for forgiveness and the offended party. The same applies to courtship. Indeed, perfect love would never hurt the one loved. But none of us is capable of perfect love for one reason: we are imperfect. Although we do not know how flawless perfection has to be. The Bible makes this clear to us. The ability to apologize when wrong is a great virtue and a major pillar that sustains a relationship. You must be willing to apologize each time you are wrong. This is something we assume you are aware of, but just in case you do not know, kindly take note of it. Healthy courtship is not dependent upon our perfection, but they are dependent upon our willingness to acknowledge our wrongs and ask for forgiveness.

By and large relationships, as I (Dr Oyeniyi) have experienced, require getting to know that tolerating a person is limited. Maintaining relationships requires accommodating the other person. The understanding and acceptance of our different upbringings will go a long way in helping you develop the capacity to accommodate. Accommodation stems from developing an emotional resistance to the dark side of our loved ones.

We might never get a chance to meet with all our readers in person, but in this book we have met. We pray for you already and we are sure of Gods awesomeness. So, believe and you will have an awesome courtship that will lead to 'forever journey with the one you love.'

Perhaps you haven't given your life to Christ, here is an opportunity for you to allow Christ into your life., *I invite you into my life to be my Lord and saviour. I say bye to the Devil and World, please wash away my sins and write my name in the book of life. Keep me standing in you till the end."*

If you confess that, we congratulate you, we advise you to find a Bible-believing church and commence worshipping with them, take the believer's class, and other classes that would groom you in faith.

REFERENCES

We acknowledge some books read on Courtship; whose principles serve as a guiding principle for me in my relationship. Gary Chapman (Four seasons of Marriage, things I wish I knew Before Getting Married, Five Love languages, Five Languages of Apologies), Pastor Kingsley Okonkwo's sermon, and his book on Seven Questions Wise Women Ask. Dr Daniel Olukoya (Dancer's at The Gate of Hell, Your Marriage and Your Ancestral). Pastor Greater Oyejobi (Christian Defect). Pastor Oyejobi Kayode (Common Errors in choosing a marriage Partner) and Oba Dr Adetoyese Oyeniyi. JP Thank you for your counsel always.

We say thank you for providing insights